Love Precious Humanity

The Collected Wisdom of Harry Palmer

Kayt Kennedy, Editor

The hope of future generations is the chance we have to awaken in ourselves a consciousness that is increasingly immune to irrationality and that values wisdom.

—Harry Palmer

Love Precious Humanity: *The Collected Wisdom of Harry Palmer*
by Kayt Kennedy, Editor

Published by
Star's Edge International®
237 N. Westmonte Dr.
Altamonte Springs, FL 32714
USA

tel: 407-788-3090
fax: 407-788-1052
e-mail: avatar@avatarhq.com
website: www.starsedge.com

ISBN: 1-891575-23-6

Cover and original art: Jim Becker

Printed in the United States of America

Star's Edge prints on recycled paper and uses
soy-based inks whenever possible.

To Harry with eternal gratitude. I cannot imagine what my life would have been without you and Avatar®. Thanks to you, I don't have to.

—Kayt Kennedy

Table of Contents

Foreword

I started collecting the wisdom of Harry Palmer, creator of Avatar, in 1989 when I first took The Avatar Course. I found these bits of wisdom scattered throughout my life: on dog-eared index cards, on odd scraps of paper, on napkins, in the margins of my various course study packs. I finally consolidated all the bits and pieces onto the pages of a legal pad. It felt good to have everything in one place, but it was still not convenient to find the quote I was looking for, nor was it convenient to carry with me. I decided to compile and categorize and index my collection into book form, knowing that many in the Avatar network—and many who aren't—would take pleasure in having Harry's insights, revelations, and advice in a compact, portable form.

We are blessed to have this wise and unassuming teacher in our midst, one who assists us in recognizing our belief systems for what they are, in dismantling the ones that no longer serve us, and in creating ones that will lead to balance, harmony, and greater joy for ourselves and for our planet.

Perhaps you will find some of your favorites in these pages. I trust that you will find—as I have—gentle reminders for living life deliberately.

With love,

Kayt Kennedy

Appreciation

1

Appreciation

Appreciation is a combination of understanding, quiet amazement, and gratitude. Appreciating something permits its experience and integration.

The only things that burden or define us are those things that are not appreciated. In the presence of appreciation, desire and resistance transform into knowledge.

Appreciation

To begin the process of sorting out
your life, you must own and appreciate
the circumstances you find yourself in
right now—continuously.

Stress results from an unwillingness
to experience a creation. Relaxation is
restored by an appreciation of the
creation.

Attention

5

Attention

The word attention is derived from
the Latin *ad tendere*, meaning to stretch
toward. When you put your attention on
something, you stretch your awareness
toward it.

❧

Peace of mind is not produced by
pleas or supplication, but by achieving
command of your own attention.

Attention

Attention, like gravity, holds things in place by drawing them toward its source. The character of what is attracted is of no concern to either.

Attention solidifies a belief into a reality.

Attention

Interest is fueled by free attention.
Obsessions are fueled by fixed attention. You can intensify your interest by
supplying more attention.

Attention

Surprise is receiving an impression contrary to what you programmed your attention to look for.

Gravity particles create mass. Attention particles create identity (self).

Attention

The proper use of will power is not conquest and subjugation, but the disciplined control of your own attention.

∝

Certainty is total faith. Faith is a super-concentrated attention that solidifies a belief into a reality.

Avatar

11

Avatar

The mission of Avatar in the world is to catalyze the integration of belief systems. When we perceive that the only difference between any of us is our beliefs, and that beliefs can be created and discreated with ease, the right and wrong game will wind down, and world peace will ensue.

With Avatar everyone wins. Every person who becomes an Avatar shifts the collective consciousness toward greater tolerance and understanding. Helping yourself with Avatar helps everyone else at the same time.

Avatar

The purpose of the Avatar initiation is to transform the seeker into the polisher.

Because we are not denunciates, the Avatar teachings are exchanged for money, but our love, care, kindness, and advice are free.

Avatar

Avatar is a path to truth that doesn't begin with a lie.

As Avatars, we remember who we are and who we are not. We remember we are not things. We remember we are not any of the ideas of nationalism or race that humans fight over. We are neither expressions nor identities. We are the source of these things, and we can create better.

Avatar

Religions are revealed teachings.
Philosophies are deductive teachings.
Avatar is an experiential teaching.

The truth that an Avatar Master
teaches does not require a name, for it
does not pass through the world, but
is the loving model of willingness to
share consciousness.

Avatar

As Avatars, we want to be responsible
for creating ourselves, not just for getting
to a point where we can live with ourselves. We're creators, not adjusters.

Awareness

Awareness

The mantra of awareness is not Om; it is Aaah!

Awareness and consciousness are not the same. Awareness has an adimensional quality about it that is beyond existence or not-existence. Consciousness is fueled by awareness. Awareness is like the electricity that powers a computer.

Awareness

The heart of unmanifest awareness can be reached by successively discreating all *as perceived by* definitions, all *I am* creations, and finally, all space.

At its highest possible level, awareness is simply the urge to create.

Awareness

Awareness illuminates reality. Those things that reflect awareness are desired; those things that absorb awareness are resisted.

Karma is a ransom paid for the return of awareness.

Being

Being

You are much deeper, much broader, much brighter than any idea you could have of yourself.

In regard to being, your most effortless definition is closest to divine.

Being

Being is a more fundamental condition than existence.

If you assume a level of being that is expansive enough to contain the universe, then the universe is within you.

Being

Expand responsibility broadly enough, and you are always dealing with a self-stimulating closed system.

Never was there anything outside of you. Never shall there be. The infinite expressed, a celebration to discover, YOU are the ONE.

Being

I am is easily overwhelmed by adjectives.

Definitions, concepts, ideas, and thoughts may be extinguished, but not undefined being. The Upanishads say, "If a man fails to realize undefined being before he casts off his body, he must again put on a body in the world of created things."

Being

What a fabulous moment, to realize
that no word or thought can truly
describe you.

The world is a reflection of me.

Being

As your own true nature is realized—undefined and ever present—all will recognize that there is no gain that we do not all participate in and no loss for which we do not all share the sacrifice.

When you adopt the viewpoint that there is nothing that exists that is not part of you, that there is no one who exists who is not part of you, that any judgment you make is self-judgment, that any criticism you level is self-criticism, you will wisely extend to yourself an unconditional love that will be the light of the world.

Beliefs

Beliefs

The beliefs you truly hold, the ones you've decided to believe, your faith, will cause you to create or attract the experiences which will verify them.

How much a belief affects reality is determined by the measure of certainty with which it is held.

Beliefs

What we believe and how we believe determine our reality.

Beliefs are the thoughtforms through which we create, interpret, and interact with reality.

Beliefs

When you say you believe one thing yet experience something different, you are saying what you ought to believe rather than what you do believe.

It's easier to observe what people believe than it is to have them tell you.

Beliefs

Pretending is imagination without faith. Creating is imagination with faith. When you believe in your pretenses you create them for real.

Personal reality reflects what you really believe—not always the same as what you may be pretending to believe.

Beliefs

You experience what you believe,
unless you believe you won't, in which
case you don't, which means you did.

What you know becomes a belief as
soon as it is expressed.

Beliefs

You may believe anything you please, and when you decide to believe it without doubt, it is what you will experience as your personal reality.

Knowing is another word for believing without doubt that you are right.

Beliefs

The beliefs that you hold, whether deliberately chosen or indoctrinated, create a model for interpreting and structuring reality.

Beliefs are seeds that will one day flower into realities.

Beliefs

To make something real you must believe in it. For it to be real to others, they must believe in it.

Something is complex only to the degree that it does not fit with what you already believe.

Beliefs

Beliefs create separation between self and the universe. This is me. That is that.

When you change your beliefs, your experiences will change.

Consciousness

Consciousness

Have you ever seen a clown who pulls
a silk scarf out of his pocket, and it's tied
to another scarf and another scarf and
another scarf until the whole floor is
covered with scarves, and there is no
end in sight? That's what it's like trying
to explain consciousness to consciousness. Pretty soon the whole universe is
on the floor, and there is no end in sight.

Consciousness did not evolve from
the universe; the universe evolved from
consciousness.

Consciousness

The Eskimos have 40 ways of saying snow—all words are a way of saying consciousness.

Sooner or later, no matter what you are studying, it will eventually lead to a study of how your own consciousness works.

Consciousness

Something is reasonable as long as it fits with the way you structure your consciousness.

Seriousness results in a contraction of consciousness.

Consciousness

There will always be as much conflict and suffering in the world as there is ignorance and fear in the consciousness of humanity.

The problems of the world must ultimately be solved where they began—in consciousness.

Consciousness

Order is established in animal consciousness by dominance. Order is established in intellectual consciousness by argument or debate. Order is established in spiritual consciousness by respect.

Desire & Resist

Desire & Resist

Desire is an enzyme that releases the energy for attainment contained in a purpose.

Peace of mind is not the result of obtaining your desires; it is the result of losing your desire.

Desire & Resist

Resisting a creation means that you will not willingly own it, experience it, or recognize yourself as its source.

Either desiring or resisting results in the attraction of the creation that is the subject of your attention.

Desire & Resist

If you resist something with enough force, you project it into the environment and are surrounded by it.

The surest way to make something persist is to resist it.

Desire & Resist

The degree of intensity you suffer in your life is determined by the creations you are identified with but are resisting.

Pretending is resisting what you decided to believe.

Desire & Resist

Desire is a resistance to being without. Resistance is a desire to be without. At the root of both is longing.

We are unable to understand the actions of another because of our resistance to being that viewpoint. This is the cause of intolerance.

Desire & Resist

Resisting identifying and experiencing yourself as the source of a reality leaves that source of reality operating beyond your understanding and control. Resistance creates new sources of reality.

You cannot change your relationship to an upset, pain, idea, or fear by resisting it. You must experience it to its limits, without resistance, before you can step beyond.

Desire & Resist

Desires. Resistances. They supply the motives that direct your life when you don't.

Ego

Ego

The ego arises when you begin to defend or acclaim the definition you have assumed.

The ego's sole purpose is to acquire attention particles from others, overtly or covertly.

Ego

The ego's primary interest is not in becoming enlightened but in receiving the praise of its neighbors.

Ego is a failure to recognize that you are involved in a symbiotic system.

Ego

The ego is fundamentally concerned with calculating its own imagined advantage.

True spirituality offers no benefit to the ego—only extinction.

Enlightened Planetary Civilization

Enlightened Planetary Civilization

If you fired an arrow, stopped it in its flight, and sighted along the arrow, you would see where it was going. If you stop life in flight and sight along it, you will see that it is headed toward an enlightened planetary civilization.

Your biggest contribution to an enlightened planetary civilization is that you believe in it. The most powerful tool you have is your faith.

Enlightened Planetary Civilization

The first contribution you make to an enlightened planetary civilization is the example set by how you live your own life.

What is the real work to be done on this planet?...It's to make ourselves more aware, to remind ourselves that our essential nature is nonviolent, and to increase the amount of compassion and cooperation on the planet.

Enlightened Planetary Civilization

The vanguards of an enlightened
planetary civilization are often pulled
back into the masses by slanderous
criticism and rabid condemnation, but
in the process the masses inch forward.

Anticipate and begin to celebrate
the dawn of an enlightened planetary
civilization.

Enlightenment & Evolution

Enlightenment & Evolution

What does enlightenment mean? It means you stop thinking of yourself as a limited, defined individual. It means that your self interest becomes so broad that it contains all facets and all viewpoints of life.

The desire for personal enlightenment is an obstruction to its attainment.

Enlightenment
& Evolution

Enlightened beings do not create out of fear or need, but out of the sheer delight of sharing and evolving.

Secrets separate you from the unity of life. Secrets separate you from your own enlightenment.

Enlightenment & Evolution

Taking Darwin out of the equation, that which survives best is that which enhances its survival partners. Not competition, but cooperation. Otherwise evolution would end with the appearance of one undefeatable brute.

The best preparation for understanding humankind is to begin by imagining that you are a sociologist from an enlightened extraterrestrial race who is studying human evolution and development.

Enlightenment & Evolution

You are all travelers in time, each entrusted with a fragment of some evolutionary map.

Soon you will evolve and to the greater universe announce, "I am ready to play."

Enlightenment & Evolution

Confusion and enlightenment are the only states that will sustain themselves without any effort.

Philosophy is the exploration of consciousness by consciousness. It's thinking about thinking. It's the difference between a disciple and an enlightened man. A disciple is thinking. An enlightened man is watching.

Experience

Experience

Experience is being present, without definition, expectation, or judgment, with your own thoughts and perceptions.

Experiencing means you stop thinking and start feeling. Thinking is a continuous creating to avoid experiencing.

Experience

Experience is the opposite of create.
You experience your way back to source.
If you attempt to create yourself back to
source, you work against yourself and
create identity.

One of the curious things about this
universe is that if you create something
and you're not willing to experience it,
you keep right on creating it. It will
wait for you! However long it takes!

Experience

You create possibility by believing yourself into it, and you dissolve limitations by experiencing yourself out of them.

The penalty for accepting the viewpoint that your experience with the world is the source of your beliefs is that you become a creature burdened by limitation and surrounded by challenges to survive.

The prize of experience is perspective; everything else is just information.

Experience

Believing defines realities, and experiencing dissolves realities—that is the cycle of creation.

Creation is a cycle that begins with believing and concludes with experiencing.

You deserve to experience your creation of you in all its wonder.

Experience

This is the mechanism behind the idea of karma. Whatever we create, we will eventually experience. The intention with which we launched the creation will determine the suffering or joy we perceive as associated with the experience when it comes around.

Experiencing is the recovery of your own intention.

Fear, Doubt, Boundaries & Limitations

Fear, Doubt, Boundaries & Limitations

Fear is a belief in your inadequacy to deal with something.

Fears compound when you look to others to supply what you believe you must have but cannot create.

Fear, Doubt, Boundaries & Limitations

Seriousness is the experience resulting from a belief in (or fear of) difficulty.

You wouldn't be stuck in the middle of something if it wasn't just absolutely the most fascinating thing you could imagine.

Fear, Doubt, Boundaries & Limitations

Assertions hide fears of inadequacy.

Scarcity is a learned fear.

Fear, Doubt,
Boundaries &
Limitations

You are bound only by your decision
to have boundaries.

Without a definer, nothing is defined.

Fear, Doubt, Boundaries & Limitations

A limit can be either a frontier or a boundary.

⁓

A state of confusion always exists just beyond the limits of your comfort zone.

Fear, Doubt, Boundaries & Limitations

The easiest way to change something is to change your viewpoint.

Doubt is a conflict between new decisions and old decisions.

Fear, Doubt, Boundaries & Limitations

Source has no limitations that it does not choose, no freedom that it does not create.

Feeling

Feeling

Getting real is the honest, nonverbal answer to, "How do I feel about this?" And there are no rules about how you should feel.

Things become complicated to the degree that symbols are substituted for feelings.

Feeling

People who have the purpose to feel *create*. People who have the purpose to avoid feeling *think*.

Feel life. Life is.

Feeling

The purpose behind any action is to feel something or to avoid feeling something.

The reopening of perception and feel is the impact of art. Good art pulls us back from an intellectual world of words into an actual experience of the world. It brings us back to life.

God, Gratitude
& Grace

God, Gratitude & Grace

The simple reason we cannot understand God is because God is that faculty that understands—not the object that is understood. Faith and feeling alone recognize God.

God does not have to be reasonable, logical, or fair, but it is best to create her that way.

God, Gratitude
& Grace

According to some, the creation of a God is a surrender of personal responsibility for our own minds. According to others, the creation of a God is the first sane thing we have done with our minds.

Gratitude opens a crack in consciousness that lets grace in.

God, Gratitude & Grace

Grace is always here, and we receive it to the degree that we are open to it. When we're desiring or resisting, we're not open. No grace, separation, suffering.

Many people spend a great deal of time seeking gratification but almost no time experiencing gratitude.

Happiness & Love

Happiness &
Love

Happiness is an intentional creation of the self universe: *I am happy.* Of course, the self can believe in all sorts of appropriate reasons for making itself happy or unhappy, but the bottom line is that the self decided.

You know what will make you happy in this world? Nothing. Pursuing, possessing, or protecting any "thing" doesn't work. You're unhappy until you get it, and then after you get it, you're unhappy when you think you might lose it.

Happiness &
Love

You collect it, and then you protect it.
Those go together—collect, protect.
When you're protecting, you're not
happy.

Happiness requires that you restore
inner peace.

Happiness & Love

Seek happiness where you lost it.

If you wish to experience happiness, be happy. Only a fool waits for the world to make him happy.

Happiness &
Love

Each moment that you are happy is a gift to the rest of the world.

Love is an expression of the willingness to create space in which something is allowed to change.

Happiness & Love

Love precious humanity. Seek happiness in the relief of others' suffering.

Unconditional love is a nonjudgmental, serene acceptance of the flow of the universe and an unshakable faith in the good intention of the creator.

Happiness & Love

To a far greater extent than common knowledge would lead anyone to believe, people's happiness, health, and success are not determined by the thoughts, ideas, and imaginings they have of themselves, but are determined by the ability to change these things.

In loving someone for the way they are, you allow them to grow into what they may become.

Happiness & Love

Because your existence in time and space is unique, there are lives that only you can touch.

Honesty & Dishonesty

Honesty &
Dishonesty

Honesty is the measure of your willingness for others to know your actions, your thoughts, your feelings and your intentions. Anything that reduces this willingness separates you further from source.

Becoming more honest with yourself means introducing more honesty into the collective consciousness of the world, and this lays the foundation upon which an enlightened planetary civilization can be built.

Honesty &
Dishonesty

At the bottom of every dishonest act is a belief about your own inadequacy.

Being honest is really a question of courage—courage enough to face what you fear.

Honesty & Dishonesty

We are all dishonest as long as we do not compassionately work to correct the collective dishonesty in the world. How?…each of us, in our personal lives and dealings with others, must set a courageous example of honesty.

Honesty is a path that leads to peace of mind.

Honesty & Dishonesty

Becoming honest is an act of self renewal.

It is uncomfortable to be around people with whom you are afraid to be honest. It appears that they steal your source, but the truth is that you give it to them.

Honesty & Dishonesty

No amount of punishment or humiliation is worse than the suffering you create for yourself by being dishonest.

Reputation is important to people who cannot honestly look at their own intentions.

Indoctrination

Indoctrination

Indoctrination is dominating someone with beliefs. It's eating a mind.

The goal of indoctrination is to structure someone's consciousness in such a way that there are certain beliefs that the person is unwilling or unable to question. This is the way it is!

Indoctrination

The more uncomfortable you feel about questioning something you believe, the more likely that you are dealing with indoctrinated information.

Judgments & Anger

Judgments &
Anger

Judgments are what cause experience to be painful.

The harsh judgments you make about others are about the same things you resist recognizing in yourself.

Judgments placed on a creation cause it to be either desired or resisted.

Judgments &
Anger

Connecting with someone means to temporarily share their viewpoint. Connecting is an inflow of the other person's viewpoint. It requires that you suspend judgment and listen with neutral attention.

Anger obstructs the discernment of right and wrong.

Judgments &
Anger

The first step in handling anger is to realize that it is not out there; it is in here. Nothing abates anger as quickly as confession.

As a rule of thumb, the intention with which you do an action is the same as the interpretation you place on the action when it is done to you.

Life & Living

Life & Living

Your life is designed by you as a higher self—relax and enjoy, experience and grow!

Birth and death are the experiential boundaries of one brief aspect of life.

Health is an indicator of the alignment and efficiency of your society of cells. Every cell is alive and is able to work in cooperation and trust with other cells. This suggests traits for a healthy human society: trust, respect, appreciation, and cooperation.

Life & Living

What is the meaning of life? Life is. It doesn't come with a meaning.

The miracle is not that there is life within the universe; the miracle is that there is a universe within life.

Compassion and consideration, even when they do not seem to have an effect on another, release healing and calming forces in your own body.

Life & Living

If all life began its journey from one point, some going north, some east, some south, and some west, and the time arrived when life was again to rejoin itself in wholeness, the path would be south for some, west for some, north for some, and east for some.

The conditions of your life should be read as a message that you are sending to yourself.

Life & Living

When events repeat themselves in my life, there is a lesson I need to learn.

Surrender is not a bad thing when practiced at the right time, but surrendering all the time is not the way of an Avatar who has also mastered the art of steering his or her own life. Learning when to steer and when to surrender is the artistry of living.

Life & Living

The ultimate in awe is coming face to face with the incomprehensible, over-whelming mystery behind life—not physical death, which the trained seeker may watch without attachment—but the actual disintegration of being teetering on the brink of awakening to something that is so tremendous in its breadth and scope that our own suffering cycles of existence are irrelevant. To those who have experienced this awe, religious indoctrination is an intellectual lullaby: "Go back to sleep."

The Mind

The Mind

The idea of achieving a quiet mind has been around since the dawn of self-awareness. It winds its way through all spiritual practices as a preliminary step to enlightenment or liberation. Shrines induce it with reverence for the profound. Whispered prayers and sacred rituals echo its importance. Monasteries nurture it through isolation and reverence. Legions of holy men and yoga teachers have invented techniques for its attainment. Why? Because a turbulent mind is an obstacle to spiritual practice.

Refrains in the mind repeat because they were recorded during a more present moment than the viewpoint is now experiencing.

The Mind

There are three steps to achieve a quiet mind: You must 1) willingly accept and responsibly experience yourself as source of all your mental creations, 2) learn how to turn off the creation of new thinking at the source, and 3) have an effective technique for discreating the echoes of old thinking.

The purpose of ceremony and ritual is to concentrate thought and increase its influence on the mind.

The Mind

Procedures can be formulated to modify any function of the mind, but the ultimate procedure returns control of the mind to the being.

The fewer secrets we have, the more flexible our minds become.

Motivation

Motivation

Motivation is a sustained inner energy source that enables a person to deliberately act to overcome obstacles.

Inspiring someone is awakening a viewpoint that realizes that something that seemed impossible can actually be done.

Motivation

If you wish to participate in life with any degree of deliberation, your primary action must be to set a goal.

A motivated action is a sustained effort aligned with a purposeful intention.

Motivation

What you think of as an impossible dream might be reasonable if you thought differently.

Awakening, in a sense, is realizing there are other possibilities.

Motivation

Compartmentalize your life. Don't allow those areas where you are having difficulty contaminate those areas where you are doing well.

Envy is an enemy of cooperation. Sincere congratulations melt envy.

Past, Present & Future

Past, Present & Future

The past would not exist if it were not being created in the present moment.

We do not, as some psychological practices would have us believe, drag the past around with us. We create it moment to moment as it serves to support our beliefs about what the past ought to be.

Past, Present & Future

Perhaps the least obvious thing about our past is that it is over. It's done, finished, completed, and cannot be changed. Nothing in the past can be undone. No one can be resurrected, punished, or consoled. The door is closed, and it will not be opened by any entreaty.

The past influences us as long as we let it.

Past, Present & Future

The past is not the source of the present; the present is the source of the past and the source of the future. It's all here, right now.

The past and the future do not exist unless we deliberately (or by some default process) decide to create a memory or image of them in present time.

Past, Present & Future

Everything that exists is being created right now.

This present moment is the beginning of time.

Past, Present & Future

When we move away from being the source of our beliefs, the inertia of the past takes over as the source of our beliefs.

Others may not choose to be free of the past and may continue to project past identities upon you. This must be endured until your actions cause them to reevaluate the identity that they thought you were.

Past, Present & Future

Realize that in this present moment you are exactly where you once decided you wanted to be. There is no point in second-guessing the wisdom behind your decision. It made sense at the time.

The past is an idea we create in the present.

Past, Present & Future

Enlightenment is the discovery of eternity in the present moment.

Present time is a creation whose limits lie within the present moment.

Reality

135

Reality

Reality consists of the experiences
you believe are real. What is real may
or may not be the same for everyone.

Reality is anything you believe it to be!

Reality

Understanding that you create your own reality, you learn to experience it as devoutly and as respectfully as any blessing bestowed by any Infinite Creator.

Reality is now, and it begins and ends with you.

Reality

The entrance door to a reality is that you believe, without doubt, that you can experience it.

Fantasies are the possibilities of experience that people believe are not real.

Reality

Certainty is not a body of information; it is a decision that creates an experiential reality.

Just as adding a single drop to the ocean causes microscopic changes in the volume, the temperature, and the currents, every time an individual changes his or her beliefs, the blueprint by which collective reality unfolds changes.

Reality

All possibilities of reality exist simultaneously, and it's your choice which one you choose to focus on.

Responsibility, Trust & Agreements

Responsibility, Trust & Agreements

If you find something that you can't seem to discreate—a persistent mass—it is because it still has a source of creation energy (inertia from the past or someone else's primary) that you have yet to assume responsibility for.

If your goal is to change an event or remedy a situation, the place to start is with the portion that is your responsibility.

Responsibility, Trust & Agreements

Responsibility is being source right now. Blame is looking for who was source.

The fall from innocence and grace begins with, "I am this. I am not that." This statement is a denial of full responsibility and begins the process of defining yourself as something other than pure beingness. It is the beginning of duality.

Responsibility, Trust & Agreements

When you assume responsibility for your life, you will begin to appreciate the wisdom of all your creations, and you will find in them empowering lessons.

It is better that you denounce Avatar a thousand times than to use it even once to justify your actions. Champion no cause above personal responsibility.

Responsibility, Trust & Agreements

It is a dangerous proposition, but responsibility to humanity is above responsibility to the self. It is when you begin to act out of responsibility to humanity that forces are released that transform, in a very favorable way, your life.

Those who raise too many issues of trust probably should not be trusted.

Responsibility, Trust & Agreements

The ability to accept and honor a trust without any enforcement or supervision builds self esteem.

An agreement is the offspring of two or more minds. It has a life of its own, a developmental path that leads to a manifestation as physical reality. Once made, it cannot be turned off or discreated by a single viewpoint...It can only be changed by a new agreement by the same minds.

Responsibility, Trust & Agreements

Broken agreements trap attention in the universe of others.

Breaking an agreement drops you into the pretense of victim, locked in a struggle with an unyielding secondary, which is really only your abandoned agreement.

Self & Self Realization

Self & Self Realization

The idea that you have of self is what separates you from source. Source is undefined.

A self is an idea that awareness is availing itself of for the purpose of experiencing certain other ideas. It's the bubble from which you view other bubbles.

Self & Self Realization

Self realization is about taking control of who you allow to influence your private universe.

Self realization is knowing that you are, and operating as, the sovereign lord and creator of your universe.

Self & Self Realization

Regret is a break in higher self trust.
You stop trusting that your higher self is
creating the experience that you need
for your own evolvement.

The purpose of turning the mind off
is to discreate the idea of defined self.
This is the benefit of a good night's
sleep.

Self & Self Realization

There really is no such thing as transforming self. Real self never changes. The transformation is always in that which has been mistaken for self.

As we mature spiritually and recognize the emptiness and impermanence of self, we move beyond the goals of self-improvement and self-empowerment and embrace selfless service to relieve the suffering of others.

Self & Self Realization

Ask someone, "How do you describe yourself?" and the answer gives you a good idea of what they think about most.

Spiritual Practice & Wisdom

Spiritual Practice & Wisdom

The purpose of spiritual practice is not to become an expert in any ritual or practice, but to really experience who you are.

If you really want to practice spirituality:
1) Be honest about something that you were formerly being dishonest about.
2) Take responsibility for something that you were formerly blaming another for.
3) Treat someone whom you formerly felt superior to as an equal.
4) Use an advantage that you formerly used to gain something for yourself to gain something for another.
5) Communicate sincere congratulations to someone whom you formerly felt envious of.

Spiritual Practice & Wisdom

Surrender, as a spiritual practice, works only when it is done so completely that even the surrendering is surrendered.

True spirituality is not about ultimate rewards; it is about a daily inward experience and appreciation of existence.

Spiritual Practice & Wisdom

Spiritual practices should not be taught to unawakened consciousness; the practices will become twisted to justify cruelty.

Enlightened teachers recognized very early that presenting advanced spiritual instruction to unprepared disciples was harmful both to the disciple and to the practice. To the unprepared disciple, the advanced teachings engender pride and arrogant abuses of knowledge. Such disciples become manipulators of others, cult gurus, and not only cut the cord of their own spiritual advancement, but profane the instructions for others.

Spiritual Practice & Wisdom

When the initiation turns into ritual, indoctrination replaces realization. Concern with the performance of the ritual creates the pious ego. Repetition leads to habit. Habit leads to unawareness. Unawareness leads to ignorance and intolerance. Ignorance and intolerance lead to cruelty and inflexibility. Religion is born.

Turning happenstance circumstance into a spiritual practice has led to some pretty strange religions. I eat cabbages, because that's all the garden would grow; therefore I am following the will of God. Eat cabbages.

Spiritual Practice & Wisdom

Wisdom is the cumulative result of enduring many vulnerable moments of not knowing.

Anything that does not contribute to someone's spiritual attainment is at best trivial.

Spiritual Practice & Wisdom

Flexible wisdom gets used; inflexible wisdom gets framed.

Wisdom is like stiff clay; you have to work it with your own hands before it becomes useful.

Spiritual Practice & Wisdom

Following another's path leads to who they are, not to who you are.

The real answer to *Who am I?* is the awakening of enough self-determinism to ask a more interesting question.

In anything, but in spiritual practices particularly, not knowing does not equal ignorance. Not knowing that you don't know is ignorance.

Spiritual Practice & Wisdom

Only a few beings ever have the option or inclination for exploring genuine spiritual practices. These are domains that demand certain attitudes and qualities of character as rights of admission. These attitudes and qualities can be deliberately developed with Avatar and, in retrospect, will be considered the only thing in life that was worth developing.

Attachment to stuff is self-sabotaging to the quest for spiritual freedom.

Spiritual Practice & Wisdom

The best meditation teacher I ever had told me to think of meditation as the opposite of achieving—disachieving. Just get comfortable, she said, and spend a few minutes disachieving.

Recognizing the imperfections in our past actions inspires our future spiritual development. This is the positive side of regret.

Don't let what you are being get in the way of what you might become.

Strategy & Power

Strategy & Power

Power is the ability to remain present and aware and to shape reality.

Live deliberately is an urging not to let the physical universe or other people dictate the design of your private universe. Wake up!

Strategy & Power

It is best to consider an action in terms of its appropriateness or inappropriateness rather than in terms of right and wrong.

Resorting to force is a failure in strategy.

Strategy & Power

An individual, an organization, or even a civilization will continue to grow strong as long as it has clear, inviting goals. When it engages in actions that are not aligned with its goals, it begins to die—first spiritually, then mentally, and finally physically.

Power that is used only to acquire more power creates fear.

Strategy & Power

Make wrong is one of the last strategies that a losing competitor employs against a winning competitor. It is an attempt to associate the fruits of victory with guilt.

Enemies whose attacks fail to discourage you are soon discouraged themselves.

Strategy & Power

Determination is a quality of the heart and the mind. It should not be profaned by stubborn words or demands.

Time is created to compensate for your loss of power. When you have sufficient power, you won't need time. You will be present.

Strategy & Power

The best strategies do not require repeating, but result in a self-regenerative creation.

Getting real is about being sincere. Sincerity is the alignment of actions with intentions.

Strategy & Power

Right conduct is satisfying your basic needs in a deliberate way that does not lead to future condemnation or regret. Right conduct does not threaten anyone else's basic needs (present or future). Right conduct communicates a recognition and respect for the other. Right conduct is a gift of opportunity to others.

He who does not recognize influence is.

Success

Success

One of the things that is missed by most purveyors of self-centered success courses is that they themselves have graduated out of merely working for their own advancement and are now motivated to see others succeed.

Purpose determines strategy, strategy determines power, power determines production, and production determines success.

Success

Commitment is backing up your primary with action. Undertake something!

Expectations are fulfilled in ratio to sincere effort.

Success

To ignore what you perceive in favor of what you think or what someone tells you to think will soon have you perceiving nothing but your own thoughts. This is a prime source of failure. You can't hit a home run by swinging where you think the ball ought to be.

❧

The primary skill of successful people is the ability to control their own attention.

Success

The major things that are keeping you from greater success are the unknowns in your own mind.

People who mistake instruction for criticism, or vice versa, remain ignorant.

Success

For any question beginning with "why" the answer is "because"; for any question beginning with "can" the answer is "yes."

⟡

Use any abundance that you create to support and accelerate the self-realization of humanity.

Success

There are only two modes of operation: Whacking at the Beast, meaning making progress, and Celebrating Victory. When we are certain of success, we don't need to wait until the last minute to celebrate victory.

Suffering

Suffering

The best way to remove suffering from your own life is to act with the intention to reduce the suffering of other sentient creatures.

The fundamental ignorance that drops you into an existence of suffering and struggle is forgetting the lesson: This is not-I; this is my creation. The fundamental ignorance that drops you into an existence of aggression and anger is forgetting the lesson: Just like me...

Suffering

The punishments of mind and man
are inconsequential in comparison to
the obscuration of spiritual illumination
that secrets and deception cause.
Humiliation, fines, imprisonment,
and even execution are preferable to
a wasted lifetime of suffering.

The real benefit of forgiveness is that
you discreate any effort within yourself
to cause another suffering.

Suffering

The question to ask of yourself is,
Why are you? The question is not, *Why
am I?* Asking *Why are you?* of yourself
creates a viewpoint that links you with
your creator. The inevitable suffering
of personal self is transformed into
the recognition of life lessons that
contribute to the broader scheme
of things.

Engaging in harming another solely
to prevent harm to yourself is a greater
harm to yourself than anything you
might have prevented.

Suffering

No one can make you feel or think in a way you don't prefer unless you let them.

Abandon concern with what happens to you, because what it happens to is not you. And to what is you, nothing ever happens.

Truth & Lies

Truth & Lies

Truth, should you ever wonder, is
an alignment between what you are
creating and what you are experiencing.

What we look *as* and where we look
from determine our perception of truth.

Truth & Lies

If we understand that we experience what we believe, and if we allow ourselves somewhat more uncertainty, then we don't lock ourselves up in one truth for the rest of our lives—a single truth makes us intolerant toward people who hold another truth.

Truth can be far more flexible than delusion.

Truth & Lies

Truth is the viewpoint of source. A lie is basically an entertainment device.

If we spoke only the truth, there would be nothing to say.

Truth & Lies

Not knowing is profoundness. It comes as close as possible to the truth. The truth is nobody knows.

A created thought creates a reality, but a response thought creates a lie. What is the lie? It's simply, "I didn't do it!"

Truth & Lies

I don't think we can speak the truth—
we can only BE the truth. Truth lies
beyond definition.

The only certain expression of truth in
any philosophic conversation is, "Yes,
that is a viewpoint."

Truth & Lies

There is no truth to know about anything until someone creates some.

A lie is an attempt to experience something other than what you are creating.

Truth & Lies

Truth is relative to the point of view from which it is perceived.

It's true because we say it's true. Everyone, from their viewpoint, is seeing truth.

In a universe based on duality, there is always an opposite viewpoint.

The World

The World

There is no reason to conclude that the perceived world is an illusion, or that it is real, or that it is anything else. It is just a phenomenon. Become as attached or as unattached to the phenomenon as you wish; just be willing to experience the consequences.

Live while you are alive. Seeing the world as illusory while you are alive is as delusional as seeing the world as real when you are dead.

The World

Every moment of happiness, every moment of sadness, every kindness, every critical thought adds its consequences to the blueprint of the world.

Notes

Notes

Notes

Notes

Index

203

Also By
Harry Palmer

Avatar®

The newsletter that was once
available only to Avatars is now
available to everyone.

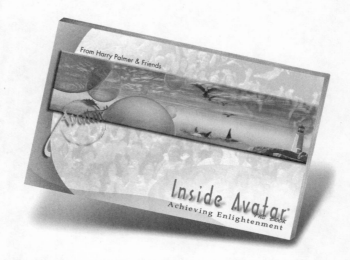

INSIDE AVATAR® THE BOOK

• What will make you happy? *(p. 2)* • What can you create by mind alone? *(p. 5)*
• How to use power without repercussions. *(p. 14)* • What is the real
lesson of need? *(p. 17)* • Take charge of your own thoughts. *(p. 28)* • How does
Avatar work? *(p. 42)* • Why am I participating in this creation of life? *(p. 45)*
• Who do you think you are? *(p. 54)* • Preserving the laws of scarcity. *(p. 66)*
• How do you handle the losses and sadnesses of life? *(p. 68)*

*Find the answers to these questions and
many more inside Avatar.*

To get your copy of **Inside Avatar The Book** contact Star's Edge. Be sure to
include your name, address, telephone number and credit card number. The
book is US**$12.95** plus US$4 domestic or US$6 international shipping.

Star's Edge International • 237 N. Westmonte Dr.
Altamonte Springs, FL 32714 • tel: 800-589-3767 or 407-788-3090
fax: 407-788-1052 • e-mail: avatar@avatarhq.com

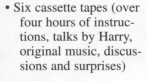

THE THOUGHTSTORM®
MANUAL

A group discovery tool that can unlock the answer to nearly any question in the universe. What do you want to know?

In the years since its first appearance in 1986, Thoughtstorm has established itself as a favorite tool of the entrepreneur. It has inspired the creation of thousands of businesses and sits on the bookshelves of some of the wealthiest people in the world. The book is deceptively profound in its ability to generate insights into the problems facing all of us.

The current edition is an extensive revision of the original Thoughtstorm package and incorporates recent research as well as a newly written chapter explaining why Thoughtstorm works.

Answering the questions in Section Two of this manual will reveal more insights and opportunities than you dreamed possible. Follow the simple instructions, meet with a few friends, and you will quickly discover the power of Thoughtstorm.

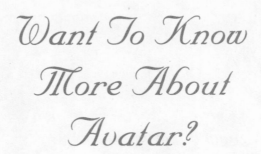

Want To Know More About Avatar?

If you would like to know more about Avatar, contact Star's Edge International.

Star's Edge International
237 N. Westmonte Drive
Altamonte Springs, FL 32714

tel: 407-788-3090
fax: 407-788-1052
e-mail: avatar@avatarhq.com
website: www.starsedge.com